American Sign Language

Food

by E. Russell Primm III • illustrated by Kathleen Petelinsek

childsworld.com

Published by The Child's World®
800-599-READ • childsworld.com

Copyright © 2025 by The Child's World®
All rights reserved. No part of this book may be reproduced or utilized in any form or by any means without written permission from the publisher.

Photography Credits
Arni's Indonesia/Shutterstock.com, cover; Tim UR/Shutterstock.com, 1, 7; Daxiao Productions/Shutterstock.com, 3; pzAxe/Shutterstock.com, 4; Markus Mainka/Shutterstock.com, 5; Jochen Schoenfeld/Shutterstock.com, 6; Max Topchii/Shutterstock.com, 8; All for you friend/Shutterstock.com, 9; primopiano/Shutterstock.com, 10; WS-Studio/Shutterstock.com, 11; Subbotina Anna/Shutterstock.com, 12; Sea Wave/Shutterstock.com, 13; Jacek Chabraszewski/Shutterstock.com, 14; marco mayer/Shutterstock.com, 15; Martin Rettenberger/Shutterstock.com, 16; Lotus_studio/Shutterstock.com, 17; Alena Haurylik/Shutterstock.com, 18; Viktor1/Shutterstock.com, 19; Shulevskyy Volodymyr/Shutterstock.com, 20; NataliaZa/Shutterstock.com, 21

ISBN Information
9781503889026 (Reinforced Library Binding)
9781503890107 (Portable Document Format)
9781503891340 (Online Multi-user eBook)
9781503892583 (Electronic Publication)

LCCN 2023950369

Printed in the United States of America

Note to Parents, Caregivers, and Educators:
The understanding of any language begins with the acquisition of vocabulary, whether the language is spoken or manual. The books in this series provide readers, both young and old, with basic American Sign Language signs. Combining close photo cues and simple, but detailed, line illustrations, children and adults alike can begin the process of learning American Sign Language.

Let these books be an introduction to the world of American Sign Language. Most languages have regional dialects and multiple ways of expressing the same thought. This is also true for sign language. We have attempted to use the most common version of the signs for the words in this series. As with any language, the best way to learn is to be taught in person by a frequent user. It is our hope that this series will pique your interest in sign language.

A special thanks to our advisers: As a member of a deaf family that spans four generations, **Kim Bianco Majeri** lives, works, and plays among the Deaf community. **Carmine L. Vozzolo** is an educator of children who are deaf and hard of hearing, as well as their families.

E. Russell Primm III was a well-known figure in the publishing industry who produced thousands of acclaimed books for children. He was affiliated with organizations such as the American Library Association, the Chicago Book Clinic, and the University of Chicago Publishing Program Advisory Board.

Kathleen Petelinsek has loved books since she was a child. Through the years, she has written, designed, and illustrated many books for children. She lives in Wisconsin, near her granddaughter who also shares her love for books.

There are 7,500 different types of apples in the world.

Apple

Make a fist and put the knuckle of your index finger against your cheek. Twist your wrist back and forth.

Banana plants are not trees—they are a kind of herb.

Banana

Motion as if you are peeling a banana.

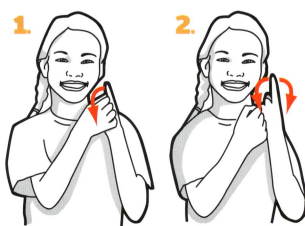

1.
2.

You can eat every part of a watermelon, even the seeds!

Watermelon

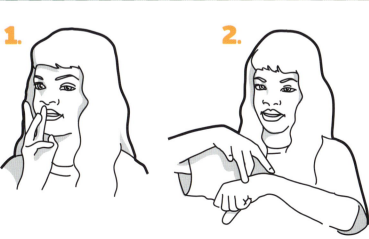

1.
2.

Make the "W" sign and touch it to your lips. Then thump your other wrist as if you are thumping a melon.

The average person eats about 15 pounds of fresh oranges per year.

Orange

Make the "C" sign and then the "S" sign in front of your mouth twice.

A strawberry has about 200 seeds.

Strawberry

Pinch two fingers and cup your hand in front of your face. Then twist and move downward.

The biggest tomato in the world weighed over 11 pounds (5 kg)!

Tomato

Flick your lips with your finger. Then motion as if you are slicing a tomato.

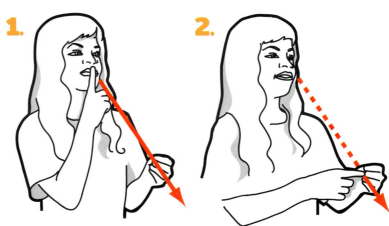

1.

2.

Corn is actually part of the grass family.

Corn

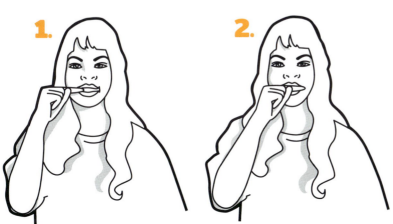

With your finger, motion as if you are eating a cob of corn, twisting and moving the cob right to left.

> Americans eat nearly 50 billion hamburgers a year.

Hamburger

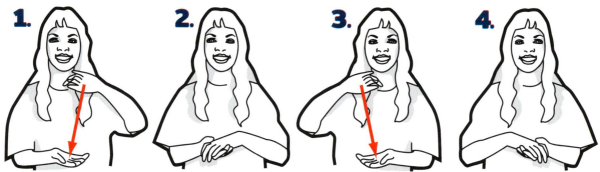

Cup your right hand over your left. Clap them together softly. Then switch. Motion like you are making a "patty" with your hands.

Hot dogs are also called "frankfurters" or "franks."

Hot Dog

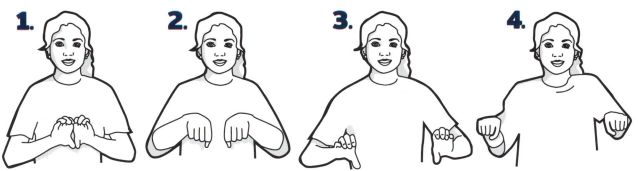

Make two "C" shapes together. Move your hands apart a bit, and make two fists. Make the "C" shapes again, then move your hands apart even more, and make two fists.

This sign for "chicken" can also be the sign for "bird."

Chicken

Open and close your fingers like a chicken's beak.

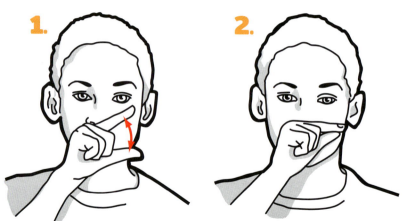

1. 2.

Chickens lay an average of one egg per day.

Egg

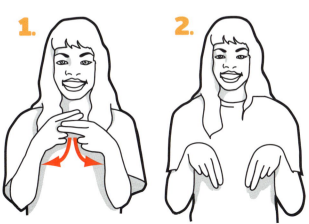

Make the "H" sign with both hands. Tap your fingers together, then move down, as if you are breaking an egg.

Trout is a popular type of fish to eat.

Fish

Wiggle your hand and move it forward like a fish swimming along.

A lobster's body does not have any bones.

Lobster

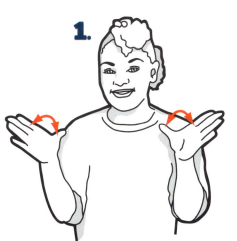

Open and close your hands like a lobster's claws.

What is your favorite soup to eat?

Soup

Cup one hand like a bowl. Use two fingers of your other hand to scoop toward your mouth.

1.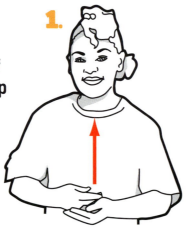
2.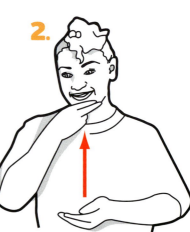

The main ingredients of bread are flour and water.

Bread

Your left hand stays still. Curl your right hand slightly and motion as if you are slicing bread.

Cherry, apple, and pumpkin are all popular pie flavors.

Pie

Pretend to "slice" two pieces of pie on one of your hands.

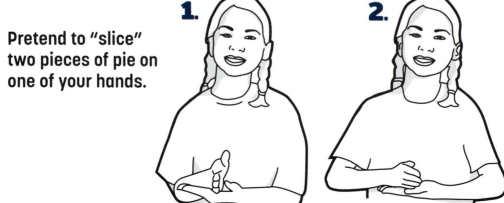

Americans eat about 20 quarts (almost 19 liters) of ice cream a year!

Ice Cream

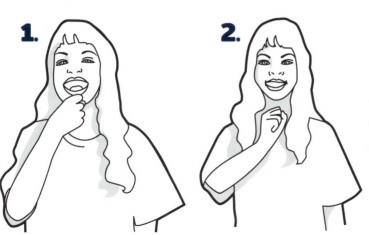

1.
2.

Make a fist and move it in front of your mouth as if you were licking an ice-cream cone.

Just smelling chocolate can make some people feel relaxed!

Chocolate

One hand is palm-side down. The top hand makes the "C" sign. Make two circles with your top hand, as if you are stirring chocolate.

People have been making cookies for over 2,000 years.

Cookie

1.

2.

3.

Make a loose "C" shape. Bring it down onto your other hand. Bring it up and put it down again, as if you are cutting out cookies.

Wonder More

- How much did you know about American Sign Language (ASL) before reading this book? Do you already know some ASL signs? What new signs did you learn?

- Some words or specific names don't have signs. In these cases, you can spell the individual letters of the word, which is called fingerspelling. Look at the alphabet chart on page 23. Can you sign the letters in your name?

- With a partner, pick three signs from this book and practice them together. Are you able to understand each other? Is ASL easier or harder than you thought it would be?

- Think of a food word that isn't in this book. Try spelling out the word with fingerspelling. Then look up the ASL sign for the word. Where can you find more ASL signs?

Sign Language Alphabet

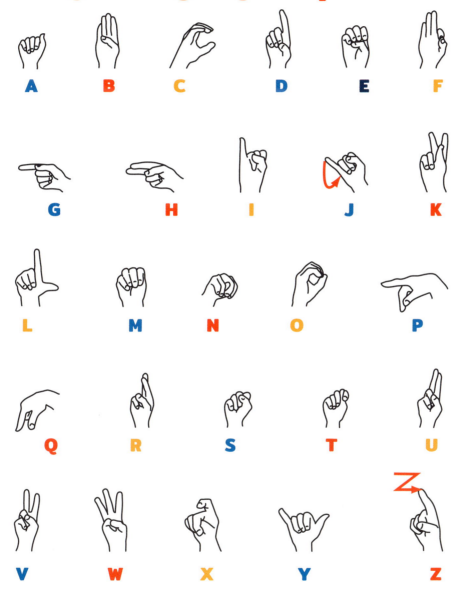

Find Out More

In the Library

Adams, Tara, and Natalia Sanabria (illustrator). *We Can Sign! An Essential Guide to American Sign Language for Kids*. Emeryville, CA: Rockridge Press, 2020.

Martin, Ann M., and Chan Chau (illustrator). *Jessi's Secret Language: A Graphic Novel* (The Baby-Sitters Club Graphix). New York, NY: Scholastic, 2022.

On the Web

Visit our website for links about American Sign Language:

childsworld.com/links

Note to Parents, Caregivers, Teachers, and Librarians: We routinely verify our web links to make sure they are safe and active sites. So encourage your readers to check them out!

A Special Thank-You!

Thank you to our models from the Program for Children Who are Deaf and Hard of Hearing at the Alexander Graham Bell School in Chicago, Illinois.

Aroosa is in third grade and loves reading, shopping, and playing with her sister, Aamna. Her favorite color is red.

Carla is in fourth grade. She enjoys art and all kinds of sports.

Deandre likes playing football and watching NFL games on television. He also looks forward to going to the movies with his family.

Destiny enjoys music and dancing. She especially likes learning new things and spends much of her time practicing her cursive handwriting.

Xiomara loves fashion, clothes, and jewelry. She also enjoys music and dancing. Her favorite animal is the cat.